Next Door to the Dead

Next Door
to the Dead

Poems

Kathleen Driskell

UNIVERSITY PRESS OF KENTUCKY

Scholarly publisher for the Commonwealth,
serving Bellarmine University, Berea College, Centre
College of Kentucky, Eastern Kentucky University,
The Filson Historical Society, Georgetown College,
Kentucky Historical Society, Kentucky State University,
Morehead State University, Murray State University,
Northern Kentucky University, Transylvania University,
University of Kentucky, University of Louisville,
and Western Kentucky University.
All rights reserved.

Editorial and Sales Offices: The University Press of Kentucky
663 South Limestone Street, Lexington, Kentucky 40508-4008
www.kentuckypress.com

Library of Congress Cataloging-in-Publication Data
Driskell, Kathleen Mason.
 [Poems. Selections]
 Next door to the dead : poems / Kathleen Driskell.
    pages ; cm
 Includes index.
 ISBN 978-0-8131-6572-1 (softcover : acid-free paper) —
 ISBN 978-0-8131-6574-5 (pdf)— ISBN 978-0-8131-6573-8 (epub)
 I. Title.
 PS3604.R56583A6 2015
 811'.6—dc23
                                    2015014667

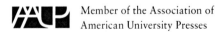

In Memory
Pamela Papka Sexton
1946–2014

Contents

Part 3

Part 4

Ars Poetica

Most headstones are covered with green and purple
lichen, ruffled frill humble as cabbage,
so ancient they can only be read with fingers,

but, besides those, there are the more recent graves dug
by men with long hair and cigarettes, shovels, and yellow boots
while I have watched from my laundry-room window. How is it

I have come to take carrion comfort looking out over all resting
in the little churchyard next door? No matter. With this dark
   nourishment,
imagination, my only god, lifts, takes wing.

Part 1

In Praise

For the doe hit a week ago, knocked dead
to the cemetery culvert, I praise the buzzards
for coming out into the sleet and darkening day,
when the roadman would not. Praise
the greasy black prayer-circle, forgive
their unctuous attention. And the dark congregation,
a dozen or more who roost in the bare branches
of surrounding trees and praise to those at the outer
limbs who keep wait like feudal sentries
in worn-shine coats. All ready pallbearers
who will lift high the deer into the grave
weeping sky. But I'm also grateful for the one
in particular who has come to squat atop
the humble lichen-covered monument
of Sarah Blakemore, who had birthed six children, all
dead and lain before she. My highest praise is sent
to this dark angel of brief ornament.

Living Next to the Dead Acre

The preacher who sold us the old church
    said *Pshaw! Ain't nobody been buried there*
in years, no fears, that little cemetery's been full
    up long ago, but we'd only lived there a month,
were still washing dishes in the ladies' room
    sink, when I drove home in sleet to find
a hearse, its doors agape, brass handles
    on a casket, the casket sliding out.
I slid in behind the long row of cars
    and parked as if I belonged there. I did
my best to hush the rustle of grocery store bags,
    to hush my kid trying to kick free
from his car seat. He bleated to be
    let loose, to be allowed to join that party.
I held him so tightly he yelped.
    At the tall vestibule doors, I struggled with
and cursed my new sticky key. Behind me
    small purple flags flapped in the wet wind,
banners pronouncing the new patriots
    of this strange country.

Funeral, in February

Across our lawn, black
coats moved as if
they were the heavy
notes of a dirge.

The Mower

I.

Before his twenty-year-old son was laid
to rest, the only lawn he'd ever mown
was his own. Now, nearly every week
he wakes us from our Saturday sleep.

The muttering riding mower comes
up the road, a slow moan growing
louder as it closes. For more than an hour,
he goes round and round and round

and if you've ever mown a yard with fruit
trees and a swing set and a fire pit
and a swimming pool that sits above ground,
and a fort that threatens collapse,

you know it's not an easy task.
There are many things to steer around
and many things try to shut the motor down
and bring the sharp blade quiet.

And no matter how close the mower shaves
around impediments, a green live fringe
circling each monument remains, won't be
edited out, can't be cut to the ground

without the weed-whacker's extra labor,
which in the mower's hands reminds, somehow,

of the old-timer's patient work with the scythe,
though this gas motor leaves his hands

shuddering for hours after he returns home
to his dark place, where he sits at the table
and brings hands to his face.

II.

At Jason's grave—

always other things: a Wildcats flag,
a blue sash that reads *This We'll Defend,*
a solar light that blinks at night, a tawdry
bouquet of plastic yellow tulips.

Each week, it seems, something new
is found, something new to be borne,
something else to cut around.
And, then, she, too, who comes late

and creeps in to grieve. Once the mower cut
his engine and leaned over our picket fence
to talk. It was she, he said, who had sent the ruined
boy up the ramp and into the black mouth

of the Army's transport plane. After she goes,
often, I walk out to see—to witness—what she's left
behind, what next Saturday the mower is sure
to pitch up atop the high pile of clippings and rubbish.

Child's Poem for Sgt. Horace Mitchell Jr., 1946–1968

War is bad.
It makes me sad.
When my uncle gets home
from Vietnam,
I will be glad.

Consolation

Here my son my only son my boy
a good boy he was
helpful to all even the young
woman stopped by the side
of the highway her tire blown her
blond hair blowing in the wind of
passing long distance haulers the one
who hit him and kept moving as my boy
fell hard into his temporary grave that deep
roadside ditch where only a thin trickle
of water ran but before he landed oh how
my boy flew through the air
like an angel my son the one the one
who died for beauty

Ars Poetica

Given enough time, they will come . . .
          they always do,
lifting one by
          one into

                    the air
                              like kites
in a worried wind.
          They wear the white nightclothes

                    of moonlight.
Some are tethered
          to their headstones.
                    They fly highest.

          Some have long knotted tails

                    that swish
                              and whip from side
to side in the squall, angry.

Some are small.
Some are so

                    small they look like knots of white
and the wind is unkindest to them
                              for they seem so unsuited to flight.

Some are tied to unmarked graves
                    and are more listless, seem
          to stutter
     across the purple grass.
                              Why
          they seem tied to
nothing, nothing
          but their narrative—

          (or to mine).
                         They pull against restraints
               and all strain
                         to break away, to float into
                    their heavens, but I awakened
                    in the night again
     and again stand
          at the bedroom window.

     Behind me,
husband softly snoring,
               dog, softly snoring.

     My fingers on the cool blue silk

          of curtain. Like a sultan
who has clapped hands, twice, quick,
     I have summoned them
               but hold them
                              in the low sky
               above the churchyard.

                              Moored, they tug against

my greed,

          my imagination.
     I know I could let
          them go,

                              but

no, not

     yet, no.

Mounds

Not only the living are weighted
with regret. Clearly, the recent dead
don't rest easy in their graves either.
What else would cause them to put
their shoulders against the pine,
to push out and push up, as if trying to
force open a door blocked by drifted snow?

What Haunts

Their headlights wake us, beams moving slowly
up the hill as if lanterns lit and swaying in
the hands of a mob steady in pursuit of scent.

When the light shines through our bedroom, I know,
without asking, that my husband's eyes are open
and when car doors slam, wordless, we both creep

to the window to watch them float across
the little graveyard next door. They hoot, howl,
chest-bump, bellow, stagger, and weave through

the stones, red tips of their cigarettes flitting
through air like laser light, beer cans catching
moonlight, seeming to hang airborne on their own.

All this we watch, satisfied to stay
unseen, until a hulking form vaults up
onto the headstone of Aleta Shallcross. *Hell,*

no, my husband growls, watching the form ride
the marker like a surfboard, laughing when
it cracks, falls over. My husband's gone then,

already bolted out the back door, out,
into the black; then, his voice shoots
over our fence. They stop still like a herd,

stunned. I can feel their ears twitching, and then
comes the prickling moment when I wait
to see whether they will scatter, scramble

to their cars, shriek away, tires squealing
back down the road, dissolving again through
the dim door of night, or, with bared teeth, raise

their sniffing noses to catch the scent of
my husband, standing alone at the edge of our yard.

Epitaph

For the Blue Ribbon Baker

She was not afraid of the grave—
on the green earth she had
accomplished much, after all,
a wall full of county fair ribbons
and engraved plaques, all won
for her rich buttery shortbreads
and frosty pink cakes, and still
she knew her greatest reward
would come when, like a yeasty
hot cross bun, she'd rise up
and float as if angel-food into
the arms of golden-haired Jesus.

Infant Daughter, Marcus 2 Years Old, Myra 8 Days

Among these tiny grave markers, I think of my own
little terrorists, my budding suicide bombers.
They shriek against inoculations, squirm, refusing
the spinach on their plates, try to swallow marbles,
run from the care of the woman who is
CPR certified. They smile when they see me
watching their plump fingers fingering the cord.
Every day, with such joy, they threaten
to blow apart my heart so utterly.

Markers

The oldest, 1848. Memorializing a mother
and infant engaged in the same grave.

The newest, a teenaged girl, crushed in a car.

I had come out to hang my laundry on the line,
to make it sweet in the first balmy sweep of spring.

I pinned up the corners of my blank white sheets,

and watched her father, who had come alone to dig
the hole in which to bury her ashes. Fabric tugged.

All pains. All pleasures. All things so

divinely human. Defined, yet also
infinite, at rest in between. And heaven above

waiting, heaven, that blank to be filled in.

Part 2

Epitaph

Jesus Called and Wanda Answered

Let us think of Wanda
next time our phones ring,
breaking our moments
of noses in good books.

Let us remember
Wanda, who, were she still
living, might have said,
"if I hadn't answered the call,
would I still be dead?"

Next Door to the Dead

I say it as if I might run over
with an empty cup
to ask Mrs. Luck for some sugar,
for surely long-lived Mrs. Luck
(1818–1898) was fortunate enough
to grab something sweet to take with her
into the grave. I say "next door" as if
it's a place I might call upon for a needed egg
or a length of green thread.
"I'm going to walk next door," I call,
and my husband understands
I've gone to visit our nearest neighbors,
to walk among the one
hundred and twelve headstones,
planted thus far.
                          I never plan
to knock, wouldn't want to
intrude, don't have time to
come through any door—
though I suppose that's what each
lying here said, when he or she
dropped in to visit the dead.

Pathetic Fallacy

Through the rippled fields of the neighbor's farm,
    they mosey, loose-hipped,
looking downward, downward, as Prometheus wished.
    Their noses scrape across
the stubble of grass. Their noses lead them
    until one seems surprised
to find she's drifted to the cemetery fence.
    Bequeathed, she reaches through
and pulls at this greener grass. Chewing slowly,
    she seems now to be
considering the headstone just in front of her,
    her jaw moving side to side
like a metronome. Her tail swishes away
    the flies, but she seems to be
mulling it all over, to see into the earth
    and down into the old crumbling coffin,
which holds a human skull, forever looking
    up, which is also as Prometheus desired.

Lament for the Crow

Here lies black crow.
I stumbled upon him
a few minutes ago,
resting in a cradle
of long soft grass.
He is as sleek
and neatly tucked
as a chrysalis
I studied in school.
The blue and purple
shimmer has not ungleamed
from his wing
and sleek head. He has not been
dead long. My ears catch
the sky, and I turn my chin
up to see his kin,
sifting down, one by one. Some
settle upon branches
of lofty trees. Some
twitch and coo. Some are still
and stoic in their dark
coats. Some rock back and
forth, unconsoled. Like
humans, they confront
the open grave in their own way.
I scarcely know how long
I've been motionless before
wings in the trees begin

to flutter and, observance
ended, in one rush
the flock re-launches.

Just Off Shore, the Shadows Move

Slim sea trout swim
just beneath the Irish Sea's
surface. From the cliff,
I can see them twisting
in water the color
of church glass, as if
they are the newly buried,
not yet admitted.

The Egyptologist Speaks from the Grave

I thought my shadow
was my soul.
When I saw it
behind, I knew
to think about
where I'd just been.
When I saw it beside,
it was my friend,
my comforter.
When it led me,
I followed.
But down here,
it has abandoned
me, no light, no
shadow, no soul.

Inishmor, Aran Islands

I see in myself what could not be seen
until considering these squared green fields:
the rolling land has been caught, seized,
fenced by its own stony elements.

Tchaenhotep

Mummy at the Kentucky Science Center

I.

Excited flurry of bees,

striped in khaki and blue,

they swarm from the school bus doors

and up the stairs to surround me,

palm prints on the glass,

nose smudges on the glass;

they think I am

a goddess,

immortal, and you, teacher,

lingering behind,

your face against the glass, too,

as if it is a church window,

what think

you of me?

2,500 years ago, in my hot kitchen,

a star exploded

in my head.

As I lay there

    I smelled bread

        burning in my oven.

    That aroma still wanders

    through my emptied veins.

    By the time the miller came home,

        he found me dead,

but I was not yet unspooled into the heavens.

    I watched from the rafters

        as they carried me out,

    as the miller gave over all his grain to the priests,

        as the embalmers filled me with salt and herbs,

    as I was washed with wine,

        as I was left in a dark tomb

in the Valley of the Queens.

    You see there,

             teacher, on my plaque,

    I am no goddess.

    I was no queen.

I was a housewife,

middle class, very

        pretty it was said, but

    no queen.

And did I ever once lay myself in the miller's coarse arms

    and sigh for immortality? It was not for me

        that he gave everything

        to have the priests

        wrap me in linen finery.

            Into my cold ear, he whispered

                talk sweetly to Osiris, bid him

                to let you open heaven's door for me

                when my time comes.

                    For thirty years, each noon,

        the miller shielded

his eyes and looked up, hoping

        to see me traveling

                in the sun's fine painted boat, gliding
                across the sky.

He did not know

        that for centuries I lay in the dark.

        II.

For two thousand years, I practiced my ritual confession:

I have done no evil against any man.
I have not done that which is hated by the gods.
I am not a worker of wickedness.

For two thousand years, I waited for the door to open,
                and when it did, the sun lit
but another pyramid on the stone wall.

        III.

        Finally, I crossed water.

    I rocked across the blue for weeks
and when we docked, I thought I'd come to heaven's gate.

Again, I practiced my recitation.

I am not a murderer.
I have not snared the birds consecrated to the gods.
I have not taken fish from holy lakes,

but no one asked me to speak,

I was only told to be

        still, here, there,

                faces and faces leaning in

close, their sour living breath blowing over me.

        Why be a god if you are but a thing

                to be so coarsely regarded?

        IV.

I did float in a river of death, once. You, teacher,

            tell the children

      how the great floods of 1937

            rushed into this city, and how the water rushed

upon this city, and how the water rose against

the marble walls of my gallery, how giant

           fishes with the snouts of crocodiles swam all around me,

until I finally spilled out of my stone coffin

            and how, though the waters were rough,

I floated like a thimble, peacefully,

            down Liberty, down Broadway, down Market.

            Would you believe me if I said

        I thought the gods of the dead

                had at last summoned me?

        V.

      Never mind. Do tell the boys how my head

separated from my shoulders—boys like

            hearing such things—but don't

tell the girls how I watched myself float
apart,
so that I could see most clearly
how I had been overcooked all these years,
had turned into something that looks
                    moth-eaten, dark like dried fruit.

I was promised that when I revisited earth, I would be
                    a yellow bird,
                              a red-winged beetle,
a blue feather rocking
        gently in the wind.

                                        They all lied.

VI.

I have not been called because I cannot say:
I have not caused men to hunger.

Teacher, how the miller chased my maiden
skirts around our kitchen, hot hearts
of household panting together in that dark place,

my husband's heart was lean
and stringy. He eyed me as if I were something to eat
and he was a wild dog on the streets.

Have you, like me, had to make your heart a pillow,
a place for a man to lay
            his head after love—

is that why you linger? Do you understand
            to lie next to
                        a man who always wants to enter you, can
            make
                        any woman want
to close the doors of her own body—still,

                        to roll a boulder across the opening
            of a body brings another kind of death.

VII.

My head bobbed in the flood's current

like an old jug, but how I traveled!
                        I heard the oars cutting the sun-boat's
                        path in the water!

            I have not turned aside the water.
            I have not put out the fire when it should burn.
            I have not prevented the temple cattle from grazing on my land.

But the notes of the water music came from an unpainted boat.
            Paddling, two boys, not much older than your students.
                        What's that? one boy said.
I saw a soft white face lean over the edge.
                        I don't know. Fish it out, called the other.
Oh, my gosh, they both said, realizing
                        they had brought in not a fish,

but a head! My head rolled, returned to my coffin
and lay in my arms for years until
I was stitched back together.

Like Frankenstein
a little boy once said
as he was reading my museum note
to his mother.
They turned away, disappointed, they had hoped—
I was something grander than I really was.

But what am I, what was I ever, but a thing
that has been made
and now is condemned
to float forever
in this glass boat of accruing
animal knowledge?

Love Poetry

When Dante Gabriel Rossetti
presented his manuscript,
a culling of his best love poems,
to his adored young wife,
placing the loose, crackling
papers on her breast as she lay
unmoved and hardening
in her casket, his falling tears
loosened the ink of the words *love*
and *pain* and *icy crystal cup*.

Seven years later, an itch—
full of regret, sorry he had not
made copies of the originals, he paid
four copper coins to have her
dug back up. The two scruff-bearded
men with shovels were amazed
they had not been asked to recover
a family emerald or gold ring,
but instead were requested to
bring back only fusty papers.

And while digging, they surprised
themselves by unearthing thoughts
of their own wives, their long marriages.

One man began to hum a hymn
without knowing why; the other raised
his chin and barked at the sky.

It began to rain hard in London.
Rossetti stood by the fogging window
and watched the wet street
for the men's return. Despite
the storm, it was a good day
for those who had been parted.
While all know the lesson
that life must go on, a few had learned
so will love, and, others
had learned, so must art.

Epitaph

For the Grave Digger

Here lies ol' thin Pete, who, for once,
got to stick around and meet those
at the graveside, instead of hiding
out in the dark wood beyond,
his back against a lichened tree,
wishing the weepy folk were gone
so he could shovel it all back in
and head to the widow's with enough coin
to buy some stringy rabbit meat.
Here's one grave ol' Pete won't
ache from refilling.

Night

Upon the little
acre of earth, night's
heavy bucket tips

its spill. Darkness's edge
leads with greasy
lips. Rising like

the Lethe,
medicine water swallows
each gravestone.

Death of the Civil War Infantryman, Mill Springs, Kentucky

In the cold mud, oozing, I lay. Looking up. Into
the weir, the fingery reach of wet tree branches. One
glides down. Then another. Another. What? Red birds—
cardinals—light on limbs. The sky. Gray. Infinite.
Approaching. Each bird, sudden, unexpected, like
sudden blood blooming through the chest. A flock
has settled in the tree. They are. Like Fanny's precious
red glass bulbs. They came from Cincinnati
on the river boat. She held them in her lap. A small
raw wooden crate, stuffed with straw. *Careful, careful.*
She warned. The slow nod of the horses heads out front.
Heading for home.
Clicking, I hear ticking like a clock.
Expensive. Foolish. But pretty. Glass glittering
in a leafless tree. Leafless. Tree. Through
the sleet, a song—sad. So sad. No—
not a song.
The low moaning of our messiah.

Part 3

The Death of the Snake Handler

He was buried with his good book
and a canvas bag cinched tight,
where within were the remains
of the snake

that left two oozing gashes
in the preacher's cheek.
As he lay dying, he accepted
it was God's will,

but still
asked his deacon to separate
the snake's head from
the coiled noose of its body,

to show the snake
that in the end, he was but a worm
in the world of men,
and the snake,

before the hoe's head fell,
hissed *then surrender, please,*
only a worm was needed
to bring you to your knees.

Epitaph

For Colonel Sanders

Here lies old Harland who was
buried as expected in his starched
white suit, his black bow tie
in a limp loopdy-loop, one hand still
gripped around the polished knob
of a hickory walking stick.

Above him now, his tomb noble
as a king's ziggurat. Oh, fried chicken
laureate, Ozymandias's demesne
was no more significant. How smart
you were to retail each spicy secret!

Cemetery Irony

Yellowing plastic tulips do last, perhaps longer than
a lifetime, and so remain to perpetually say,
I love you and miss you, but only in an artificial way.

At Harland Sanders's Grave

"and his wife,
Claudia,"
the inscription reads
at the squat base
as if they'd said,
fuck it, let's just
throw her bones
into this old bucket.

Too Late

Long after innocence, that pink nipple,
yields to the wet mouth of experience,
one blunders, almost indifferently,
over the line. Slowly comes the comprehension,
that now, no longer is there fear of dying
young—or even the romance of thinking
one might die young. Instead, sluggishly,
the worry awakens. It is possible,
one begins to understand, to die too
late, handcuffed inside oneself.

The moon—the lunatic moon—hangs
in the window. Clumsy executioner,
ham-handed, it drags its dull axe behind.

Border State

And in the far corner, two untrue
rows of rock nubs, as enigmatic
in their pattern as a tiny Stonehenge.

Otis, the grizzled trustee, points to say
they're the graves of the Whittles' slaves.

But Marta, his bent wife, shakes her head.
Kentucky Lutherans, our people, staunch
abolitionists, *freed Negroes*, she said.

Epitaph

For Uncle Joe, the Slave

Here lies ol' black Joe, a good obedient
servant to the end. He loved us as if
we were his own kin, and we did right by him,
and gave him Jesus whom he wouldn't have known
from Adam, had he not been bought and brought
to Kentucky when he was but a tar-baby
of two and just weaned from his mother.
There's no birth date for his stone,
but his death date is known and will be
duly recorded in the family's ledger.

At the Grave of the Girl Slave

Little girl who lies beneath
this stub of stone
among this wreath
of enigmatic markers,
below my feet
perhaps you lie
straight bones unstirred,

except for the ossified
fingers collapsed and fallen
like toy soldiers
through the battlefield
of your hollowed chest,

your crossed hands
having melted from
their well-mannered
pretense, that same stance
you were ordered to assume

after being called to
the big house that hot afternoon
and lined up in front
of the steep porch steps to be
shown to the stranger.

     Or . . .

perhaps below my feet,

your hands rest still
at the end of long thin bone,
mummified into clench,

because your mother said no
to those who tried
to position your prayer
hands within the box
and instead she
reached in and took
yours in hers
one last time
and molded each
into a tight fist

so that you were lowered
into the ground
defiant, so

that when you met
your maker
he would know you
were pissed

and had some things
to say and settle before
you walked through
the swinging gates
of paradise, crusted
with false pearl and bliss.

Epitaph

He Never Killed a Man
That Didn't Need Killing

Some lines, after all, shouldn't be
crossed and here lies a man
who'd be damned if he'd let
anything or *anyone* stop him
from standing his ground.

Infant Girl Smithfield

My mother
looked at me,
then turned away.

The midwife tried
to hand me
to my da

who shook his head
to say he would not
like to hold me either.

Her rough hands
that swaddled me
were quick
and competent,

and took care to tuck
my blue toes
snug within
a little blanket, soft

and clean

and newly knitted pink

and embellished with rosebuds,
leaves of green,
and bustling honeybees . . .

but those hands were not
related to me

and neither were
the hands of the man
who lay me
in a narrow box

into the grave he'd dug
no deeper than
his knees

and who with his shovel
had already begun
to return the dirt
over top of me

when the preacher arrived
and jumped off
his slumping horse
and quickly said his words.

I saw into his withering heart
and knew he thought
he'd come too late
to save my infant soul.

No matter. For now
I sleep, soothed within
the loving arms

of my opening rose
and rest best next to

my blood, my beloved,
my five brothers
and six sisters.

Just As

Why are the smaller stones
    so weighted?

Were not those graves filled
    with souls equal to all others?

From the Grave of the Mathematician

Alive, I would have celebrated the proximity
of all these etched numerals, little pluses
in crosses carved in stone. How I used to
love them all, the sprawl of figures turning
across the blackboard, and yet to me these
past eight and hundred years have been marked
by the inelegant unyielding square and square
and square squared. Neat edges cut
into the earth by the shovel and the gravedigger's
boot. How differently, lying here, I've come to
understand the slash of a grieving man walking
against the winter wind and the equal signs
that wagon wheels leave in the mud
when carrying an infant's coffin.

Mt. Zion, 1918

After another long rough wagon rolls away,
the heads of the teamed horses nodding *ya, ya, ya,*
down the rutted lane, the young preacher settles
into the chair in his small study, looks out
his window over the churchyard, lifts his pen
for a moment. Outside, eleven new graves, each
red Kentucky hillock, a testament. He dips dark ink
and begins: *my father, you who judged so harshly my exodus*
from our Virginia farm, cursed my leave-taking,
the family break in our land-owning lineage, if only today
you could be here—with the help of this divine blue flu—
see you here what all I have sown, grown,
and then harvested for the belly of our great Lord.

Part 4

On a Walk

In the clearing, I stumble over
the deer skull yet unbleached from the sun.

A black trail of ants enters the socket of one eye
and goes out the other, emptying dreams of wild carrot,

low peaches, dinosaur kale, the tops of turnips,
feast to be returned to the belly of the forest.

Clearcut

After he buried his daughter's ashes,
he began to visit with a chainsaw.
Eerily, then, our weekends have filled with
high-pitched *mmmmm-mmmmms,*
as the toothy blade finds it all.

Past darkness, he downs the orphan
trees encroaching at the wild edges
of the graveyard. He piles them,
limbs heaped, untidy ricks.
Each weekend, the mound grows

as if someday he might climb those wobbly stairs
to heaven. Somewhere, though,
within the curled leaf of his heart,
that brittle place, is a place that knows
it can never be reattached to green tree.

Shunned

After he was hanged, a workaday knife
with a coarse hilt cut him down

and he was laid into a pine coffin and the dark
cooling brook of men washed beyond the boundary

of the graveyard, carrying him to that estranged
grave outside the picket fence. Despite what he'd done,

Oscar Legg was put to rest with civility.
Odd, they took such care lowering him. One man

even rolled an uneven mossy rock, a homely stone,
but perhaps that was only to mark the misery he'd caused

them all. By that time, Ellen McCain had already lain
for days within the still row of her gone kin.

She had no stone. The mason said it might be years
before her grave settled enough to set one properly.

Yet, somehow, this was a comfort. For a while
longer then, marked Ellen continued unmarked.

One Side of the Double Marker Left Unengraved

And here I wait—bracelets
of purple petals, forget-me-nots
around my wrists,
two ribs re-knitted askew,
a tooth now forever lost
to my head, wrapped in
tissue and tucked into
my jewelry box,
and instead of peace
slowly dropping, I lie—
as I did in my marriage bed,
listening, waiting, on
edge, for you to arrive,
knocking around drunk.

Epitaph

Wife of Proud Buck Shallcross

Now—and forever—here lies my Ruby,
just as she did during this earthly life.
She was a beautiful woman, but
she sassed, and loved falsely,
and the truth she refused to tell,
even when her life depended on it. Too
bad. She might have lived a little longer.

Epitaph

For the Man with No Last Name

Here lies Ned, a man
with no last name,
found by the tracks
leading to Bethlehem,
Kentucky. We know not
if he was jumping on
the train or off, nor
do we know where
he expected to end up.
We found in his coat
four gold U.S. dollars,
a pink ribbon, a woman's
chased silver ring. We,
God-fearing, buried most
with him, but not a letter
of rebuke. If your name is Bess,
and you are sharp-tongued,
and capable of sending a man
out into the wilderness
in search of his own death,
you may find your letter
tacked to that hickory
tree over yonder.
We saw no need to bury

it with this poor fellow.
Surely, it'd been scorched
upon his heart
while it still beat.

Not Done Yet

I was not dying. No, not
at all. Rather, I was lying

in bed when the corpulent fly
fuzzy-blacked past my head.

I went on trying to read, but all
I could hear was stumbling buzz.

He hurled and swung through the air
on wings in wide, swooping arcs

as if on a big-tent trapeze. *It's fun!*
he taunted, *Wheee!*

He sailed right. *Follow me!* he teased
as he looped back from the left.

My old fat dog, now blind
in one milky eye,

lunged, as if a crocodile
striking high, leaping from water

for a tasty, feathered snack.
His yellow teeth clacked

after the superciliousness!
The haughtiness! I hissed, *Get him!*

Get him, boy! Try
again, I'd urge each time

his grizzled snout snapped
shut, each time he missed

the offending black morsel.
I bristled, *Don't give us up*

yet, boy! Jump! Jump!
But then the dog felt an itch

and began to snarfle
and slitch and thump and lost

interest in the stubbly punk,
the bristly lesson learned once again,

though it seems with some we are linked mutually,
how easily a flea is swapped for a fly

and how easily a fly is swatted away,
superseded by a more biting sorrow.

Epitaph

Dear Departed Dave
He Chased a Bear into a Cave

"Dear" meaning here
"oh, bless his heart,"
which is our way
in the South
of saying *poor, poor Dave,*
he really wasn't
all that smart.

Unused Grave

While time and elements refilled
you with nothing but your own red dirt,
have you thought long on who managed to skirt
your fixed and final embrace?
A soldier's miraculous recovery
from the bluing fever of Spanish flu?

Or knocked cold by the back hoof
of an ornery mule,
the blacksmith, hair slicked neat and combed,
and in his only suit, nearly nailed
into the box but for a pallbearer
who saw a finger twitch?

Or perhaps the remarried wife,
whose last letter cut deep,
revealing she'd really rather sleep
for an eternity next
to her first husband?

Or perhaps when excavated,
you sprang a leak and your bottom
became a bay where no one wanted
to launch a loved one's final ship.

No matter. Whoever's escaped you
has now long been caught.

He or she may have found
another place, but it's only
another place to be naught.

When the Dog Went Blind

He stood in the middle
of the room and barked.

He slept with his eyes open,
unwilling to miss a thing.

Sometimes, he walked
up to the wall and whined,

as if now in his bright mind,
he could finally see the door.

Empty Grave

You want
to know?
Then, stop
here, lean
in, put
your ear
near. Never
mind that
your sneakers
might collect
red clay.
Nearer, nearer
still and
I'll tell
all. Step
closer, now,
watch for
fear that
you fall.

Up and Against the Sky

In flight, each bird,
a winged note
in this blue nave.

Flock

See how like love it drifts

           across the gray sky
      as if it is floating into port—
                  a boat that enters
        many-sailored, each leaning over
               and waving wildly toward
       shore.

But, then, the boat

        turns with the wind
      and a thousand wings

                  catch sail.

                            Ah,

        now
        like love it
      struggles to come back
           and like love it pushes on

          and then I see another
        small mass drifting in
               and, then,
        another
          —and

another,
swirling and swirling above

they are

stirring the soup of love

until they drift down
as if on a parachute—

no, they *are*
the parachute,
snagged in the branches

of trees surrounding
the churchyard.

Each branch, alive,
a visual hum, each
branch rocking slightly,

hissing a bit, each branch
like a road leading to the heart

of a town I had not known

I wished to visit.

Acknowledgments

I am grateful to the editors of the following literary magazines for publishing poems (sometimes in slightly different versions) included in this collection:

Garbanzo: "Epitaph for the Blue Ribbon Baker," "Epitaph for Uncle Joe, the Slave," "Jesus Called and Wanda Answered"; *Narrow Fellow:* "Living Next to the Dead Acre." *Pembroke Magazine:* "In Praise"; *Poems & Plays:* "At the Grave of the Slave Girl," "Epitaph for Harland Sanders," "Unused Grave"; *River Styx:* "At Harland Sander's Grave," "Cemetery Irony," "Dear Departed Grave," "Death of a Snake Handler"; "Next Door to the Dead."

Thanks also to Dianne Aprile and Julius Friedman for including "Love Poetry" in the anthology *The Book.*

For their careful reading and generous responses to the poems in this collection, I am grateful to my friends and colleagues, including James Gottuso, Keith Hall, Katerina Stoykoyva-Klemer, Karen J. Mann, and Richard Newman. I also draw great encouragement and inspiration from my colleagues in the Spalding University's low-residency Master of Fine Arts in Writing Program, especially Sena Jeter Naslund, Katy Yocom, Jeanie Thompson, Shane McCrae, Debra Kang Dean, Maureen Morehead, Greg Pape, Molly Peacock, Lynnell Edwards, and Ellyn Lichvar. The talented editors, staff, and reviewers at the University Press of Kentucky have made this publication process a pleasure for me. I am especially indebted to Steve Wrinn, Ashley Runyon, Iris Law, Mack McCormick, and Patrick O'Dowd from UPK and to Deborah Golden, copy editor, and Merrill Gilfillan, proofreader.

And then, as always, I send love to my children, Wyatt and Quinn, the joyous source of many of these poems. I save my greatest appreciation for my husband, Terry Driskell, who believes all is possible, including this book, built upon the astonishing home he has made for our family with his own hands, great heart, and boundless imagination.

Index of First Lines

Kentucky Voices

Miss America Kissed Caleb: Stories
Billy C. Clark

New Covenant Bound
T. Crunk

Next Door to the Dead: Poems
Kathleen Driskell

The Total Light Process: New and Selected Poems
James Baker Hall

Driving with the Dead: Poems
Jane Hicks

Upheaval: Stories
Chris Holbrook

Appalachian Elegy: Poetry and Place
bell hooks

Many-Storied House: Poems
George Ella Lyon

With a Hammer for My Heart: A Novel
George Ella Lyon

Famous People I Have Known
Ed McClanahan

The Land We Dreamed: Poems
Joe Survant

Sue Mundy: A Novel of the Civil War
Richard Taylor

At The Breakers: A Novel
Mary Ann Taylor-Hall

Come and Go, Molly Snow: A Novel
Mary Ann Taylor-Hall

Nothing Like an Ocean: Stories
Jim Tomlinson

Buffalo Dance: The Journey of York
Frank X Walker

When Winter Come: The Ascension of York
Frank X Walker

The Cave
Robert Penn Warren

CPSIA information can be obtained at www.ICGtesting.com
Printed in the USA
BVOW03s1455230615

405133BV00001B/19/P